Ada Unseen

Frances Presley

Ada Unseen

Shearsman Books

First published in the United Kingdom in 2019 by
Shearsman Books
50 Westons Hill Drive
Emersons Green
BRISTOL
BS16 7DF

Shearsman Books Ltd Registered Office
30–31 St. James Place, Mangotsfield, Bristol BS16 9JB
(this address not for correspondence)

www.shearsman.com

ISBN 978-1-84861-663-9

Contents

Scape

Flight

Unseen

Search Ada

Notes

for my dear great-nephew Hal, who is ten

Mathematical Science is the language of the unseen relations between things

—A.A.L.

scape

Ada at Ashley Combe

I

treble   turret
in the tree tables
shut out the light

carve the window   slit
tendrils thru loop
holes

branches hold down the
roof   prevent further rising
further decline

ivy clad   cladding
pebble dash   all fixed
knowledge of parapets

an italianate arch
held the bit
the bite foretold

long roots follow the pattern
of sand stone battlement
enceinte   are you

cable: was not this about a library of truth

robin   chit chits   midges attack
you must take your chit

II

here's a horse
plunged down from the pinetum
a hobby horse

fractured and splintered
small eyes find
smashed out muzzle

at first she preferred
a mechanical horse
        in the tack room
by side saddle

she takes the wild
Forester mare
ears permanently pricked
                        forward

elements of the design

I

a close walk
is kept close

ladies
are kept close

close by
and enclosed

a close walk is dark
with no views out

close walk planting
is closed to reveal

a dramatic contrast
sycamore and hollies obscure

holly should be retrained
laurel cut to the ground

reveal the view
in evergreen   ever blue

II

terrace overgrown
sad & pointless contrast
with surrounding hills

I am balustraded
ballast traded

terraced
with terrorists

III

      fell to view
      fell to view

            Barry power station
            opens up

      contravenes
      the EU

IV

a multitude of drives
has disappeared

a coastal path
is not a drive

and drives are drives

V

a gloomy mantle of wood covers
this steep

descending in gloom
midges in my ears

a darling journey
to Culbone

picturesque

I want the birch
white bark
white lichen

I want the fir
feathering
melancholy yew

making the call longer
and fuller
      long tail tits

trills and arias
a conversazione
converse   chatter

attend   attend   attend

the homes you want
the hospitals you want

are carefully framed
are exclosed

sun finds my face
optic nerve switched on

reaching April above the trees
blurred disc on the page
flating lens   communion

(   )

stitch floating

in my eye

buzzard

above the clearing combe

irregular hexagon

I   more than two trees skin lizard lawn dowry

II   rounded swallow points mesmeric perspective

III   two sticks for one junction do not join parallel lines
      mummee   mummy   whip   whip whip

IV   bee down   hovers over our sticks   yellow & black stripes

V   meet and divide a lost lifeline   three children marked in our skin

VI   she's waiting for me with a random roman numeral
      WAIT

hex remnant

in memory of my brother

I

something   of our irregular hexagon
     in brown leaves   —   invading laurel
pheasant rootles   sweet chestnuts
    branches crack   scurry of squirrels
so much noise   tinny bird song
     sound travels   echoes

II

querying   thin   sounds   is that you
     waves on pebbles   are you here
loud complaint   another pheasant
    wire fence to keep them in   only
keeps me out   a mouse goes under
    No unauthorised persons beyond this point

III

broken branches   play a game of
    pick-a-stick   you will enjoy
this game   in a rage if you lose
  handsome russet feathers   your quiff
you are very clever   but lack intelligence
    you are apprehensive   have no need to be

IV

at the first level   these walls and turrets

        were nothing to her   everything dis

solves   all forms   (there is activity)

      tall cedar in the pinetum   has not

dissolved   renders invisible

     the sea   brings itself towards me

V

her dream   could not be kept

     in battlements   had to be unseen

not requiring landed space   robin

     coming closer   on the laurel

over the electric fence

       into the branch stack

sign remnant

pheasant shoots up
wound mechanism

authorised
beyond
point

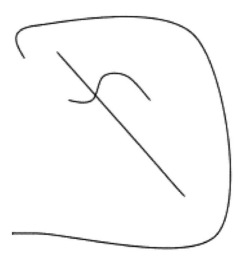

No author

passage

how did Ada walk from her bath house
on Porlock beach up to Ashley Combe
– was there a secret passage?

she did not fight her way through dead
branches and brambles or scramble up
a vertical cliff   stones and soft red earth
giving way

she did not hang on to tree roots and
branches or try to press herself against
the hill
              get closer – on all fours
but there was nothing to get close to

she did not worry   about falling
into a secret tunnel
or arrive through hart's tongue fern
finger deep   sponge moss

she did not try to find a way in through
leaf mould or broken balustrade
did not touch the wire fence
was not thrown back by electric shock

a body that falls to old faultlines
slabs   carved in the hill
white stone beach

it focuses your mind takes it off all other
problems   move more like a crab now

Typography of terra infirma

```
TTTTTTTTTTTTTTT
              T
              T
              T
               T
              T
              T T
              T TT
               T T
                T
```

T ension crack

movement on a single failure plane

since 1985

you are very concave

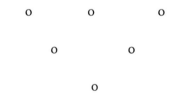

morphos of memory

tumbled ground

ravelling cobbles

                                               slip scars

slump zone

                      aprons of debris

land ÷ slip

I

stick

        points to

              rock beach

                brown sea

        points to

stick

rain

        less organised

              today

                away

          slide

feet

coast

        path for

              Culbone

                slip

          land

severe

things

        unseen

              are relative

                worthy

        because you are

it is not

someone
        has to think
                you are
                  woody
      or
worthy

holly
        cuts through
                an angle
                  right
      but not
left

petra
        falls
                against pine
                  ground
        holds
stein

cimes
        seem
                sums
                skies
        climb
crimes

bringing
        waves in
                a curl of foam
                  collapse
        waves
measure

=

branch
points
worthy
angle
waves
measure
collapse

(divide again)

land ÷ slip

II

barring
        the bath house
                     in boots
          sea dog
no

gone
          ship
                         eye
          slip
gone

light rises
          through glass
                      tintless
          window
no rose

sudden
          shelving
                      of pebbles
          in the library
sees Childe H

did your father
             start
                     offshore
             together
they are all in this

we are all

        proud of

                our fathers

        to haven

and trust

bricks

        and mortar

                fall

the board

                cedars

        breathe

did she

                        = 0

A line inflected in words

Whenever   from any point   <u>without</u> a given line

      you draw a line   to any point   <u>in</u> the given line

you have <u>inflected</u> a line   upon the given line:

Let AB   be the given line   D any point in it

                         C any point without it

            CD is a line inflected on AB

   No matter whether either CD or AB is straight

                      or crooked

     or whether they are both straight

                   or both cro

                        ked

   Again you may say that   BD   or   AD   if you like

        is inflected on   CD

         D being the point at the extremity of the line CD

The word <u>inflected</u> means literally   <u>to throw upon</u>

                       or <u>to turn upon</u>

AAB

your untenable tutor

A line inflected on a given line to Greenaleigh

A - B

telegraph wire down   below the long-fallen-tree

pale green moss & orange lichen   on the trunk

wire does not carry   does not need to carry

the familiar interrogative   of the robin

this is possible   & then again   that is possible

can I see you   or dry russet leaves

she said that her conversation   with him
was rather monosyllabic   but she meant one sided
                    monologic

here we are dialogic   you above me
                    the other further off

you ask each other what is possible

                    sharp bursts from the full throat

D

where a line is inflected
down from North Hill
on the straight gravel track
and tall beeches

a man with a white strip
either side of his trousers
and a red postbox
paused between trees
sorting post

no, at D
he is a fisherman
with serious equipment
in a red container
hoping to catch rays
or dogfish

C

climb up the hill

please shut the gate

Warning
  forest
operations

   triangle with an exclamation sign!

warning: operations

forest
forestier

   tiers of forest
   chain saw buzz

ripples of bird song
peep   peep   punctuate

A line inflected on a given line to Culbone

A - B

a given line   is loosened in the rain
                              in the sea surge
goes this far   and no further

racers hit the path   insects hit me
                              into some kind of allergy

the given line   drips down my neck
one green bottle   lies in the leaf mould

all the runners are running   they are on a given line
are marshalled

                    here is one who only half runs

no one arranges saplings   some are sliding with their weight

'If I fall over   what are you going to do?'

race marshal to greet   flagging runners
to greet me   'you ran there and back!'

C

a line inflected
on a given line
does not follow
but climbs

too many indicators:
                   Bridleway
                         points
                         in one direction

No right of way
points
in the other

the inflected line
will not carry me

no forester mare
for *Cat's scramble*

river floods
parallel
to the toll road

rotten trunk
criss crossed
by ivy stems

fly up to the sky

D

rain off the trees
to meet us

here where the lines meet
sycamore
is truer and straighter

what is the name of this river
is it Yearnor
or just a tributary

you say it is Worthy
after Worthy Combe
can you call a river Worthy

hear anything but the river
hear nothing but the river

wave function

the difficulty of measuring a wave function

           . at two specific points   separated by time .

which changes

                              continuously and causally

discontinuously and erratically

                   as a result of observation

is the collapse of the wave function

wave writing

when
waves
reclaim

shufter   shingle
                    ridge

   grey smooth stones
            white lichen

            white paint
                swastika
            on grey smooth stone
                    kick down

                    how long & when
                            waves   turn   roll
                            suck

                surf swallow
                    sink holes
                            grey   splu   sur

....

                            you pull me
                                across the breach

                tidal fast flow
                    slipping submerged stones

new salt marsh
            white egrets
                        surprised

the breach did not defeat us

Porlock Bay Nov 17

Impulse at Broomfield

I

Even the trees were adapted to scientific use: a heavy cable was
suspended by glass insulators from their branches which terminated in
the 'electrical room'

find the oak
with a wooden pole
on top

erected somehow
        – a series of ladders
        and several men

arms support   the artificial
                        limb
                        thrust in

      suspend   the   wire

generate
            more   static   on the line

      "devils dan cing on wires all lit up"

tree outlived experiment

  shakes his head
                copper bolt loose
                              walks to the lake

      saves the drowning girl with a kiss of life

oak leaves front the pole
so tight
so close

growth is from anywhere
on the oak

II

when you spread out old Broomfield on the flagstones

rooms seemed to be resolving themselves
                                    into laboratories

III

Dearest Crow

the most <u>unorganized</u> domestic system I ever saw

all seems to happen by <u>chance</u>

<u>nothing</u> is ever <u>ready</u>

        the most <u>utter</u> lack of system even in his Science

there is no <u>order</u>

        everyone straggles down whenever he pleases

nobody thinks anything of me

this is just what I want

I am a nobody here

IV

It does not appear to me that cerebral matter need be more
unmanageable to mathematicians than sideral & planetary
matters & movements... (A.A.L.)

electric currents

shot through the brain

frissions   fissions
                    hacked out

do not narrow
                            hands   vision   brain

        digital neurons flicker   and   fire

                                        − virgin soprano solo
    − choir girls   are sing- ing
                                altos in unison

who will wear rubber soles   touch the metal dome
    watch her face change   fine hair fly away

    things remembered   are harder than things forgotten

V

My dear

Many times after it became dusk did I think of your hospitable chaos

    and wish myself back

I left my gold notebook somewhere

                      if it develops itself

do not fancy   it is an *electrical*   production

                   but send it to me

flight

punch holes

I lift my conditional arm

move forward

look for

[   ]

I lift my conditional arm

move forward

look for

[a decision space]

move forward

wings

I think of writing a book of Flyology
—A. A. Byron, age 13

I am going to take the exact pattern of a bird's wing

I have already thought of a way of fixing them on to the shoulders

a pair of paper wings in proportion to my size

they might be made of oil silk   try what I can do with feathers

I can find no difficulty   in the motion   or distention of the wings

to move an immense pair of wings   take an airswallowing

     jet engine

                downstream wakes

to put serrations on the trailing edge   tattered   fringe of a scarf

     fringe feathers break up   sound waves

      velvety down feathers absorb noise above 2,000 hertz

     or change the angle at which air flows

            silent brush   of a Critch-owl's wing

      velvet coating on the landing gear

[exact]   [bird]

[fix]

[my size]

[made]   [do]

[no]   [motion]

[wakes]

[waves]

[silent]   [wing]

thrush

I fear it is a London Bird. But something better than a sparrow too

The Bird is let out of her cage every morning

She is very tame altho' of a species inclined to flights & migration

I saw 50 thrushes in 2 low cages   for sale   in Churn Passage

& they have so haunted my imagination

I am dying from a pain of thrushes

quitquiquit   quitquiquit

[fear it is]   [something better]

                   [let out]

                                                    [migration]

[I saw 01 thrush]   [rummage]   [Stonenest Street]

              [& they]   [dark spots in my eyes]

              [from a crying]   quitquiquit   quitquiquit

crow

She wants to fly into ou neck & nestle up to ou

Ou won't hurt her I think, will ou?

He is a good crow

(tho' he does try to murder his thrush now & then)

[fly into]   [&]

[hurt her]

[good]

[murder his]   [now & then]

2

we enter a bird hide & startle a large black crow

        it doesn't seem to know how to get out

clings to the wooden slats

    or waddles on the floor   like an old woman

we sit very still

crow finds the gap and stumbles out

        flies straight up and away

we say Nevermore to each other

How can a bird hide in a bird hide?   How can it be designed?

[wants you]   [with her]

[enter]   [hide]

[seem to know]

[sit]   [still]

[find]   [out]

[straight]   [away]

[say]   [each other]

[hide]   [bird]   [design]

woody woodpecker

bills for drilling and drumming   rapid and repeated impacts   protect
the brain   a small brain   repeated pecking   at high decelerations

drum rolls delivered   in under a second

O – O   O   O   O – O – O   O   O

woody woodpecker   drilling the telegraph   drilling holes in electric
poles   drilling   time tables   became   rounder   cuter   less demented

was it necessary to put on weight? nevertheless an aggressive   lunatic
no longer did the bird go insane   without   a legitimate   reason

he explained rocket propulsion

O – O   O   O   O – O – O   O   O

she slipped her voice into his audition   would not be credited   until
pecking a hole in the screen misguided missile
                                        with no language barrier

    world-wide   pecking out her name

O – O   O   O   O – O – O   O   O

plane ducks

after Escher *Day and Night* (1938)

1

ducks fly up
from the flat land
between two rivers

white ducks fly
into the night

black ducks fly
into the light

beak cuts
between wings

white ducks define
V formation

black ducks decline
<

intersect

the shape of the duck
is the shape of the field
fields are flying

wing furrows   mere ripples

wings acquire
feathers

take the dark with them
take the light with them

flying forward is flying back

2

planes fly up
from the flat land
between two rivers

white planes fly
into the night

black planes fly
into the light

nose cuts
out underbelly

white planes define
Vic formation

black planes decline
< ic

invade

the shape of the plane
is the shape of the field
fields are foils

field fin

mill roundels

wings acquire
insignia

take the dark with them
take the light with them
(copy)

flying back is flying forward

3

p

planes fly up
from the lake land
between two alps

white planes pen
       lanes
                                        black planes pen
                                      lace

                lack
                lap

white planes ace
         alps

                                    black planes neck
                                nukes

             the shape of the duck
           is the shape of the cue
             cues can caduce

(i)

dunk decal

                                      dupe drake

                deck
                  dune daps

ee up ducks

d

double

dutch

Epitaph for the Rudd- Duck

after Byron

Amber hued with bright yellow streaks
the Rudd is a Bahamian bird often heard
in a hedge shrieking   wik-i-leak wik-i-leak

The Rudd lays down large deposits
of fat under the skin and forms rectal assets of s-----
to fuel its long Atlantic flights

Known in England for mating with the native
bald-headed white screamer the Rudd once pervasive
will soon be completely eliminated

Nett Ed

Amber Rudd was a director of two offshore Bahamian firms Advanced Asset
Allocation Fund and Advanced Asset Allocation Management between 1998
and 2000   leaked documents reveal   The Fund was licensed
by the Bahamas Securities Commission and the registered agent was Citco Fund
Services (Bahamas) Limited   Citco declined to comment
    Earlier this year   Ms Rudd defended David Cameron over his investment
in an offshore fund set up by his late father in the Bahamas   Ms Rudd did
not mention her own experience of offshore investment funds but stressed that
            international transparency on tax matters is essential
    Alastair Buchanan marketed the Fund to investors and in 1999 Ms Rudd was
appointed a director of Mr Buchanan's own UK company Seaforth International
Limited
    *We worked with family offices high net worth private clients funds of funds and
private investors introduced by intermediaries   And Amber   at that point   was
a close friend   I wanted her assistance and knowledge in setting up my own show*
        A spokesperson for the home secretary told the *Guardian*
    *It is a matter of public record that Amber had a career in business before entering
politics*

Written after walking from Hackney to Woolwich

Today 9,000 passengers had their travel plans disrupted
This year 3,800 migrants died crossing the Med
By 2050 there will be 200 million climate refugees

From Hackney I walked the Greenway
along the Northern Outfall Sewage Embankment
(NOSE) into the sharp wind of Barking estuary

on Balaam Street my mouth was opened
by the Angel to bless all migrants
and drink green tea on Plahstow Broadway

As I walked by the gated Thames estates
I saw and heard the heavy planes make slow
descent to City Airport

I did not swim across the Royal Albert Dock
I did not climb up onto the runway
construct a tripod   lock myself to it

and to those who crossed the Dock with me:
Fiennes, Waldron, Pettifer, Tippet, Etchart, Grayson,
Collett-White, Lund-Harket and Sama Baka

Instead I arrive foot sore in Woolwich
drop a hundred steps down to the tunnel
where the river leaks from Newham to Greenwich

black cap

its face at first appeared surrounded   by black something

black wires   thin threads   as if growing out of the head

the head that was held   deftly between his fingers

a bird with   extraneous filaments   its dark filaments

around the head   looking out at you   and he was teasing

out the threads with tweezers   the fine mesh of the net so

hard to remove   this must be done as quickly as possible

until finally able to throw it into the sky   *where it belongs*

this face these eyes perfectly alive   and waylaid

to become tiny parcels of flesh   on a dinner plate

to be teased out   small as ovaries in full technicolour

a local delicacy

                              perfectly alive and wayward

peregrine

'Du musst dein Leben ändern' — *Rilke*

look through   a spotting scope

cathedral spire   so close   her back turned

peregrine hunches   disgruntled   damp feathers

but her face   when she swivels her neck   is bright and fierce

eyes   large and luminous

ranging   and surveillance

verify   within a mile radius

there is nothing   no part   of her   that does not see you

you must Other your life

curlew

clover embrace   curlicues   on a metal gate

buzzard   high up hover

                                 not a waver   or a waiver

clear air   sharp mountains   push

                                              aside

breathe in   for the time   it takes you   to read this sentence
breathe out for the time   it takes you   to read this sentence

do not imagine   that you have left   the slogan

                                        or the circle line

do we have another ten year cycle   try to hold her to anything

                           and she will slip through your fingers

curlew hunted by buzzard

                        wide wings

                            yellowish tip

                                buzzard pursued by curlew

curu

                    coor yew

                                   coor

buzzard flies off

                   a pair of curlews   approach

          circle & call   long after

unseen

The Fairy of Science

Science has thrown its net over me, & has fairly ensnared the fairy
A.A.L.

I

The fairies of the flowers   have been moved a decimal point
can no longer be carried over   with shrunken lungs with shrivelled
bladder campions   always the same girl   the same expression

The plant differs   the features of the fairy do not   the common
denominator fails to find the fairy of the nettle and burdock scarlet
pimpernel   byrony   goosegrass   plantain   thorn or   blackberry

Is a fairy in a mathematical system   freer   than a fairy without
the silver lady has a purpose to demonstrate an effective automaton
does not pretend to blend   with hues and pattern of leaf and flower

He wanted to place her in a book of fairies   prompted by her way-
wardness beauty and intangibility the idea of a petal with the merest
spike of a thorn not to threaten or scratch but modify mute and fade

This is her book of fairies: a fairy ensnared   in the net of science
whatever she is a fairy of the gorse flower   a fairy with a husband
of earthly clay   a fairy who fairly believes in her very imagination

2

The section of the Analytical Engine chosen for the trial was the fairy element at the heart of the machine. In fairy terms the task it would perform is trivial – a schoolroom sum. The desktop trial would add a two-digit number to a three-digit number and give the result correct to three numbers. But more importantly, it would verify a crucial element of the original design – the ability to carry fruit. The mechanism for the carriage of fruit is the most subtle and beautiful in the machine and is repeated over and over. It does not need a fairy to look at a blackboard and recite over and over or use a pencil stub to add a fruit to her sum.

3

DENOMINATED   DIMINUTIVES

    NON DENOMINATIONAL   DAEMONS

                CARRY
                        THE ONE

gorse flower fairy

'unwieldy gorse, how nearly we liken you to raiment'
Peter Larkin

you cannot shelter in a gorse bush
stand en pointe
in north wind on north hill

gorse is dense unfractured
spike through every scrub leaf
trapped in its mesh
bracken rust fronds blown across

spike bud
brown flower casing
yellowest
of yellow petals

cushion for an insect
miniature legs and wings
walking around
perplexted
between my fingers

hidden in the heart
finding the edge

spine to carry

Eden

for B and in memory of Lee Harwood

Wednesday

on Mallerstang high way   feeling wonderful
   and terrible   with sun and wind
                  looking for the source of the Eden

      this is enough for life   her life   her gift

the new guide book turns out to be a bit vague
      surely wrong about the white cottage on the horizon

                  later you will cross the gill
                  if the water is high
                  do not underestimate its force
                  you will have to turn away

you are annoyed by possibilities
            we will not know until we get there
whether to continue or turn away

                  I used to enjoy computer programming
                  telling the computer precisely what to do
                  now they interrupt you with alter
                  native suggestions with predictive spell ing

ford Hell gill
            lean over the edge of the Force
                              final fence post

            below
                  a sycamore
                        leans over dark water

                        leave the track
                        pick your way through tussock grass

clutch reeds to cross streams
                        a meadow of reeds and bog
go over my knees   water mud and slurry

a farmer above us angrily calls in
                        a stray sheep
holds his position

you must cross the last field
            climb a difficult stile
                        while I head straight for the road

Friday

on our last day in heavy rain
        we give up walking and sail Ullswater to Aira Force
                        on the Lady Dorothy

                when I was a young woman there were no viruses
                        or anything malicious
                it was creative not defensive   a faulty
                    programme   was a mistake
                                not an act of war

our little boat chases the pirate ship
                        'Drop that rope Jack lad, but not too
                        soon
                        Be careful with that rope Jack lad'
                                mocks the pirate

we start to overtake
        Jack has the hose pipe and shoots at the pirates
                        who return fire with water pistols

the pirate girl wields her red sabre
       asks if we would like to have our throats slit
              or if we prefer to be disembowelled

she is emphatic in her gestures
       and I start to fall to my knees

I want to know how we will find the right heads
when we need to glue them back on

Seven Sisters exit

for Rob Sheppard

with its long entrance subway not yet required for development   the
mosaic got very complicated and mathematical   an ellipse of a landscape
with protractors   balls of string and those enormo-sized bits of chalk
trigonometry and transportation   renamed after an English music hall
comedian   the George Robey pub in the 1980s was a venue for any up
and coming band on the toilet circuit   everybody seemed to have a love

hate relationship with the place   slipping over   someone's vomit
especially the appalling toilets   where I was plunged   by your accidental
sighting   of my heart   the only memorable musician was the fiddler
of Doom   even his highs and lows became repetitive   when you ain't got
nothing in between   its long exit subway   Cora is snacking on a pome-
granate because they always call you darling   and although she is not

dressed   in white   the underground tiles will be grouted with seeds for
at least six more years   above man height   Islington Environment &
Regeneration Department   Public Realm Division is TREE FELLING.
This tree has to be felled to enable the construction of a new development
while its hoardings incorporate schoolgirl verse /these are things you like
to see/   when you have lost the sky   got her lips got her eyes got her

fingers got her toes   there's a JCB where the stage used to be   and I'll
be there to meet you at Starbucks   renamed after the Railway Tavern
get your fresh strawberries   click out or you will face the full fare

In scena singing   there is real acting   just as on the stage   I should sing
a scena from Norma in the little library   how forcefully I can express
scorn & fury   & yet my action being all the while so tranquil

if there is a man with a mobile phone in the audience I tell him to fuck
off not mumbling no   could not pronounce her name   peri per sephone
touching the dark green tiles   her sourest Sharps   and uncouth Flats

frame

It is to me quite delightful to have a frame
so susceptible
that it is an experimental laboratory
always about me   & inseparable from me

I walk about   not in a Snail-Shell
but in a Molecular Laboratory

This is a new view   of one's physical frame

& amply compensates me
for all the sufferings

A.A.L.

open hand

this is the Ada robotic hand

from Open Bionics 3D printable this hand design

is open source and free for you to download and use

right hand components start with D for Dextrous

left hand components with S for Sinistrous

in the open hand

someone has to play dummy

and it's usually me   I'll play your hand

if you play mine with only two players

Canasta can last forever

the hand requires

a 3D palm with a chained heart line

for the highly strung who type staccato

life lines are not supplied due to re

locations and mis diagnosis

[the hand of a housemaid

is free to download by the dozen

swollen knuckles are not unprintable

can still rub a Dustface into

a tin of Black]

you have the hand

of a harpist   long fingers span

octaves   do not omit the upper notes   avoid

floppy fingers on un-optimised machines

fists bang the frame

bubble vision

(i)

if I look ahead there is a showing   a band of light rises
up from the screen   through a   head of hair   tree wigs
and a white marker   s   white   flimeering

down   don't attempt to see stitches shifting
away   or it slike the curved horizon

don't make me listen   listening b
    except to bird saong
is too forceful   am imposition

don't make me look
    with an enlarged font
or make me dictate to voie
    recognition software
all that computer can provide

Iwant eye recognisiton
    soft ware   that will speak
for me   draw for me

do not tell me to imagine my hands
on the kesy will fire syn pahses
in my brain   they are already   fired
w   were fired when my fingers ran scales
                on the back of a school chair

gove ,ue grey kewys
      give us
           through a b ubllble of water
upset the red of spell check
              I can spell if I want to

if I could find these keys   through water   through air
as something sharper breaks   over horizon
                       curve of earth rise

Retinal holes are sealed by applying buckles to the wall of the eye
which cause a scar reaction. A gas bubble holds the retina in position
until the reaction occurs. The bubble floats inside the eye cavity. As
the bubble begins to disperse, you will notice a line in your vision
that moves, similar to a spirit level. You will be able to see
above the line, but under the line the vision will be
fuzzy or blurred. The gas will eventually disperse
until it is only a small bubble at the
bottom of your eye which
will disappear too

A spirit or bubble level is an instrument designed to indicate
whether a surface is level or plumb. Slightly curved glass vials
are incompletely filled with a liquid, usually a coloured spirit
or alcohol, leaving a bubble in the tube. They have an
upward curve so that the bubble naturally
rests in the centre. This is why more
equal societies almost always
do better

The image reveals an expanding shell of glowing gas surrounding a
bright star. It is being shaped by strong stellar winds of material
and radiation produced by the star, which is 10 to 20 times
larger than our sun. These fierce winds are sculpting the
surrounding material - composed of gas and dust – into
the curved shape that astronomers have dubbed
the Bubble Nebula. The radiation is eating
into the gas creating finger-
like features

(ii)

so dark this morning in May   no thrown light or shadow
in the rush hour   loud sounds   drill the alley girls

pinning me down   two on one two on one
you have to stop   pinning me down
look what he did

the centre lamp its cut glass inscription
        all shall be well
has gone

these details of loss
            obsess him
more than any other loss

in this moment
my eye holds
anything not in its place

the window has not moved

plastic candles
            hold
    a triangle of blue lights

I cannot read the votive
        was the test done
        with your glasses on
of course it was stupid

the eye is not the window to the soul
        but a complex optical system

be in my eyes

        if you are my substance

Julian's cell
Norwich

It's estimated that three-quarters or more of the information in
the human brain
— facts, scenes, words, events, faces, places —
comes through the eyes
We literally see the world from a human perspective
Light, vision and colour dominate the living world

The siting of emotions in the body has shifted throughout history
the heart and the brain have competed as the centre of our
emotional selves
Although we live in an age dominated by the neurosciences, the
brain has not necessarily 'won out' in the battle for supremacy

Air molecules are 1000X smaller than visible light wavelengths
they scatter blue light 4X more strongly
than longer wavelength reds

(iii)

chaffinch is back   chuffed to rap
            some colour   in the rain

trying to fit file into file
                in my dream
          too many layers of fading
                coloured cardboard

white stripe wings
          flurry and return
          flurry   return

goldfinch muscles in
                muscles in

when the left eye does not talk
            to the right eye

jackdaws arrive grey scarved
            everything else scatters

perception is inference
          or was it the other way round?

return is as fast as a car
          as fast as   caw   caw   caw

everyday there is an incursion
            from the left periphery of my eye

there is an escarpment moving in
          they have removed Melmerby Fell

last late long   midsummer night
      a calling into the night and for the night

Hunsonby
Cumbria

Helmholtz agreed with Kant that the perceiver transforms what the senses provide, but believed this was based on past experiences rather than innate faculties. He was continually amazed at the way physiological mechanisms distort the information a person receives from the physical world ... and even more by the mismatch between physical events and psychological sensations (such as the experience of colour)

One might almost believe that Nature contradicted herself on purpose in order to destroy any dream of a pre-existing harmony between the outer and the inner world

Although the idea of thinking of perception as an inference problem goes back to Helmholtz, it is only recently that we have seen the emergence of neural models of perception that embrace this idea. Inferential computations are necessary for perception, and they go beyond traditional computational approaches based on deductive processes such as feature detection and classification

swimming in synch

for elizabeth james

white cross
window frames

      lights diving
       deep down
        synchronised swimmers

and so we swim again
kicking our legs in a certain
scissor routine

    program   plovers
    in parallel   position

blades of pain
      a flaunt
afloat

her spondees   enter the surface
are much bolder   in random ways

        brightening lights
         bright legs
          up ended girls

           in love
         for a girls sport
       these <u>are</u> the Olympics

capsule

for Hal

I am in the green
                           diamond panes
leaves down blow

there will be drones
                           to drown sound
to drop on a door stop

    she carries the child
    the child in her arms
    all noises cease

    held in your arms
    tightly wrapped
    legs around your waist
    he holds you

not in his immediate universe
                        which stretches
                                    to the furthest galaxies

white spots   in triangular panes
                              he will track
                                    and touch down

Julian's cell

dark matter

vast volumes of unseen stuff grip the stars

dark matter
does not shine in the spectrum
at any wavelength

there is dark matter

holding us up

there is dark matter

leached by street lights

there is dark matter

beyond the drone

dark matter sustains us

against all interference

dark matter detains us

dark matter retains us

force field

I was walking   in a field   of stars

points   of light   a force   field

     <u>non-contact force</u>   acting   on a particle

     at various   positions   in <u>space</u>

     a vector field   F   where $F(x)$ is the force

     a particle   would feel   if it were   at the point x

walking   between   the stars

you map   invisibly (x) on my vulva

Will o' the Wisp: eight equations

I

These Functional Equations are   Will-o'-the-Wisps
the moment I fancy   I have   really   at last   got hold of
something   tangible & substantial   it all recedes
further and further   & vanishes again   into thin air

A.A.L.

II

Prompted by your beauty & intangibility   you always elude
my grasp   you seem to delight in leading me   into a bog
you are will o' the wisp   flickering with wayward course
and pleased when those who follow   are bogged to the neck

Dr JK to A.A.L.

III

Lead then, said Eve   The wily adder   rolled in tangles
Makes intricate seem straight   Elevates his crest
A wandering fire   compact of unctuous vapour
Misleads   the amazed   night-wanderer to bogs and mires

J.M.

IV

God   amputates
his   small   right   hand
ignis fatuus   no illume at all

E.D.

V

A functional equation   specifies a function   in implicit form
Solve through substitution   with some constants (eg. 0 or 1)
after that some expressions
which will make some part of the equation become constant

VI

the moment I fancy I have really   got hold of
                    two or more known constants:
    marsh gas (0)   fireball (1)
it advances as you advance   recedes as you recede

VII

I have often seen it there   rising up

    and falling

                    twistering about

            rising up again

                         a candle in a lantern

                                    Mrs Lubbock

VIII

                    Joan (0)   the Wad (1)

whisp

wind on brown sedge
eyes blur on bog

if we set fire
if we light the gas

up to my waist
in water

he returns
err light

has erred
is erring

did she err
a maze of duckboard

no femme fatale
an amazement

look my dear
balls of fire roll
the gold rushes

whisps of cotton grass
you whisper

SEARCH ADA

Ada (internet cut up and paste)

for Hazel Smith

Ada is a structured, statically typed, imperative, wide-spectrum, and object-oriented high-level computer programming language. It has built-in language support for design-by-contract, extremely strong typing, explicit concurrency, offering tasks, synchronous message passing, protected objects, and non-determinism. Ada was originally designed by a team under contract to the United States Department of Defense (DoD). Ada was named after Ada Lovelace (1815–1852), who is credited with being the first computer programmer.

The Americans with Disabilities Act (ADA) prohibits discrimination and guarantees that people with disabilities have the same opportunities as everyone else to participate in the mainstream of American life – to enjoy employment opportunities, to purchase goods and services, and to participate in State and local government programs and services. Modeled after the Civil Rights Act of 1964, ADA is an "equal opportunity" law for people with disabilities.

Ada is the short form of Adelaide, which has Germanic roots from "adal" meaning "noble" and "heid" meaning 'kind, sort'. Saint Adelaide was a prominent woman of the 10th century, whose first marriage was a political union at a time of chaos in Italy. Her husband died and his usurper tried to force her to marry his son. She refused and threw herself on the mercy of Otto the Great of Germany who, taking advantage of this situation, conquered Italy and married Adelaide. They were crowned Emperor and Empress of the Holy Roman Empire. Adelaide is the patron saint of some pretty interesting things: besides empresses, princesses, brides and widows, she is also the patron of exiles, second marriages and in-law problems.

Ada, Addie and Della developed as pet forms and Ada has been an independently given name for some time. We would classify Ada as a turn-of-the-century charmer. Back in 1880, Ada was the 33rd most popular female name in America. As the decades progressed into the 20th century, Ada experienced a steady decline as she slowly fell from fashion. By the mid-1980s, Ada was no longer bestowed upon American baby girls except in very rare instances. Thanks to a new naming trend that favors old-fashioned girl names with vintage appeal, little ole Ada has returned triumphantly to the charts and she is squarely back on the American radar. Ada is a simple and quirky three-letter, two-syllable name. It's easy to say and easy to spell. It's low-key and unpretentious yet darling and "noble".

Impostor Syndrome is the feeling that you aren't actually qualified for the work you are doing and will be discovered as a fraud. It is prevalent among women in open tech/culture, many of whom have been socialised to value other's opinion of their work above their own, and to do things "by the book." Impostor syndrome is a common reaction to doing publicly visible and publicly criticised work. The Overcoming Impostor Syndrome class was created by the Ada Initiative.

Ada offers things of ink, things of ink on paper. Mostly books. Some comics. Things people call 'zines and minis and whatsits'. There are posters and prints and words on vinyl coming at you 33 1/3 revolutions per minute.

Welcome to the new look website for the Association of Drainage Authorities (ADA). Representing drainage, water level and flood risk management authorities throughout the UK, ADA also offers guidance and advice to the public about the water level management industry.

Ada met Babbage at a party in 1833 when she was seventeen and was entranced when he demonstrated the small working section of the Analytical Engine to her. She intermitted her mathematical studies for marriage and motherhood but resumed when domestic duties allowed. In 1843 she published a translation from the French of an article on the Engine by an Italian engineer, Luigi Menabrea, to which Ada added extensive notes of her own. These included the first published description of a stepwise sequence of operations for solving certain mathematical problems and Ada is often referred to as 'the first programmer'. Perhaps more important are statements that from a modern perspective are visionary. She speculated that the Engine 'might act upon other things besides number… the Engine might compose elaborate and scientific pieces of music of any degree of complexity or extent'. The idea of a machine that could manipulate symbols in accordance with rules and that number could represent entities other than quantity mark the fundamental transition from calculation to computation.

Teenage girls with an interest in computing were invited to enter a competition to mark the 200th anniversary of the birth of Ada Lovelace, generally regarded as the first 'computer' programmer. The competition asked girls: **What do you think would interest Ada Lovelace about 21st century technology?**

Ada's List is a group for women* who are committed to changing the tech industry. *by women we mean all women (trans, intersex and cis), all those who experience oppression as women (including non-binary and gender non-conforming people) and all those who identify as women.*

We're a group of 2,000+ badass people who broadly speaking, work in science, technology, engineering or mathematics. A.K.A: work in or around the internet. Digital strategists, scientists, designers, physicists, mathematicians, makers, journalists, developers, service designers, sci-fi authors, tech journalists, rocket scientists, online campaigners – if you're a woman* and work in a field related to the internet, then you have a community of peers who can help you **<u>shine.</u>**

This year, dozens of celebrations will be thrown around the world, including an "Ada Lovelace Edit-a-thon" at Brown University, where volunteers will ramp up Wikipedia entries for female scientists. Looming in the background of these festivities are findings, announced last month by the Census Bureau, that the share of women working in STEM (science, technology, engineering, and math) has decreased over the past couple of decades; this is due largely to the fact that women account for a smaller proportion of those employed in computing

Forecast for *Ada*, OH > 40.818 -83.856 > 912 ft æ Weather History for *Ada*. Ada weather Personal Weather Station

When the Gnu Ada compiler GNAT is used, the cross-reference information output by the compiler is used to provide powerful code navigation (jump to definition, find all uses, etc.).

The Tunnel Boring Machine (TBM) Ada has <u>finished building her last ring</u>, reaching her final destination underneath the heart of London and marking the completion of the Crossrail C300 Western Running Tunnels. Ada has had a much more challenging and eventful drive than her <u>sister Phyllis</u>, who finished in October 2013. Very early in her journey, Ada passed directly beneath the abutment of the Victorian era Lord Hill's bridge with only 4 metres of overburden cover. She passed even closer to London Underground's old cast iron lined museum tunnel, with negligible induced settlement. After reaching the east end of <u>Farringdon after 18 months</u> of hard tunnelling, Ada will now be encased in concrete next to her sister.

Ada is a museum of the novel, and it employs parody to rehearse its own history. In Part Five, their fantasia suspended, Ada and Van Veen contemplate their prospects for the future. Death is imagined as eternal pain, a form of madness. But word-smith Ada "know[s] there's a Van in Nirvana. I'll be with him in the depths *moego ada,* of my Hades," she says, pointing to the etymology of her name. *Ad* is a Russian masculine noun for hell. *Muki ada* are the torments of hell. "This is a … howl *iz ada* (out of Hades)," writes Ada in a letter to Van. The spirit that informs all of "Ada" is underscored by the last syllable in Ada's name when it is pronounced correctly in "the Russian way with two deep, dark 'a's" — *da!*

In 1922 on 11 November a sixty-year-old woman called Ada Emma Deane set up a camera on top of a wall near the corner of Richmond Terrace with Whitehall. From this position she took two photographs of the large crowd around the cenotaph. The first was taken just before the annual silence commemorating the Armistice and the second with a long exposure during the entire two minutes. When the photographs were developed one showed a mass of light over some of the audience while the other purported to show a 'river of faces' and an 'aerial procession of men' floating over the bowed heads of the crowd.

Notes

Ada Lovelace, daughter of Lord Byron, studied mathematics and worked with Charles Babbage on his proposed Analytical Engine: an advanced calculating machine which used punch cards and is now considered a prototype of the modern computer. Unlike Babbage, she realised its potential for uses beyond the purely arithmetical, although her example is music rather than the letters of the alphabet:

> '(it would) act upon things beside <u>number</u>, were objects found whose mutual fundamental relations could be expressed by the abstract science of operations... for instance, (that) the fundamental relations of pitched sounds in the science of harmony and of musical composition... the engine might compose elaborate and scientific pieces of music'.

Excess underlining (not always reproduced here) is typical of Ada's epistolary style, and conveys the sense of urgency, a kind of hyper-text which marks all her communication.

Scape

This section concerns Ada's life on Exmoor in Somerset and how the landscape might be reimagined through a combination of science and poetics. It was written and performed with visual poet Tilla Brading as our collaboration *ADADA:landescape*.

We know that Ada studied mathematics while she was at Ashley Combe, as well as meeting eminent mathematicians and scientists. We imagined how this might correspond to the pattern of the landscape and her life. Our arithmetic of landscape resembles Ada's description of Mathematical Science: 'the language of the unseen relations of things'. As well as using maths to create constraints for the work of literature, it also allows the landscape to provide its own constraints.

In the early nineteenth century, Ashley Combe, in the coastal woods above Porlock Weir, was described as an outpost of civilization on the edge of the vast empty wilderness of Exmoor. The Lovelace house was designed and built on a lavish scale, by Ada's husband William, in the style of an Italian villa, but surrounded by Gothic tunnels, turrets and mock fortifications. There was a large library stocked with works of the great philosophers and writers. Ada's mother had tried to ensure that the Byronic legacy was absent from Ada's life and 'this was almost certainly the first time she had unsupervised access to her father's works' (Woolley).

William also created fashionable picturesque gardens and land-scaping. Recently a National Parks report aimed to 'explore a reading of the woods at Ashley Combe as a designed landscape with a view to incorporating this design into the future management of the woodland'. We followed their field notes and responded to their attempts to restore the picturesque.

The buildings and gardens were imposed on the existing landscape to possess a view of the coast and conceal the existence of the local villagers who sustained the Lovelace lifestyle. It was an architecture of excess and social inequality. Ada's involvement in the architectural design and its execution was slight, and sometimes ironic. She preferred to go horse riding on the moor. Demolished in the 1970s, and now part of a grouse shoot, the ruins of the house and gardens are important in our collaboration, especially in the way their appearance interacts with the landscape.

pp.19–21 We drew on Ada's mathematical studies and geometric diagrams to create and write about an irregular hexagon of fallen branches near her ruined home. It gradually disintegrated and became 'hex remnant' or remnant witch.

p.23 William created a Gothic bathing house for Ada on Porlock Weir beach, which had a hidden passage up to the house. Ada wrote that she anticipated Ashley 'with delight owing to the swimming; only sometimes I fear the rocky & stony bottom'.

p. 24 The increasingly severe landslips along this stretch of the coast are caused by rising sea levels due to global warming, demonstrated by a survey in 1991. The coast path from Porlock Weir to Culbone used to lead up the cliff emerging below Culbone church: it was the path that Coleridge and Wordsworth walked, that Ada knew and that we walked until the 1980s. Now you are rerouted high up the cliff before descending into Culbone. 'Typography of terra infirma' uses geological maps from the survey which morph into a female body and slippages in Ada's life.

pp. 26-30 In 'land÷slips' a simple algorithm is used to explore the land slipped coast in which one line of verse is divided and undercut by another.

p.35–37 We mapped Ada's diagram of the mathematical concept of inflected lines onto the footpaths round Ashley Combe to create images and texts in which lines become walks.

pp.41–44 Ada visited Andrew Crosse at Fyne (then Broomfield) Court in north Somerset to discuss the uses of electricity and her own desire for a 'calculus of the nervous system'. Crosse was famous for his lectures in London on how spontaneous life forms might be generated by electricity, which Mary Shelley attended before she wrote *Frankenstein*. Ada also began an intense relationship with his son John, although their correspondence was destroyed and quotations in 'Impulse at Broomfield' are from letters to her husband William and to Andrew Crosse. It's clear that Ada loved being at Broomfield with its intellectual fervour and scientific activity, in spite of, or perhaps because of, the domestic chaos.

Flight

Charles Babbage's Analytical Engine used French weaver Jacquard's binary system of hole/ no hole punch cards, which controlled looms and weaving patterns at high speed (n.b. 'Analytical Engine' is the correct term although Ada always refers to it as 'Analytic'). In Ada's words:

> 'we may say, most aptly, that the Analytic Engine weaves algebraic patterns just as the Jacquard loom weaves flowers and leaves'.

The cards were punched through mechanically by what was called a 'conditional arm' which moved forward to look for a space and was then activated. Punch cards brought an element of choice which gave power to those who made them and the hole is known as a decision space. Conditional branching and statements are now part of high level computer programming and its instruction sequence.

Ada loved birds, especially song birds, and identified with them, giving bird names to herself and close family – she was the song thrush. Mathematics and music were her two main interests: she studied the harp and took singing lessons. It explains why her vision of alternative uses for the Analytical Engine used music as its example rather than the alphabet. In a series of poems about birds and flight, rather than flowers and leaves, I have isolated key words which might be revealed by a 'conditional arm' and create an alternative text.

p.48 When she was thirteen Ada studied the theory of flight, using the design of birds' wings and steam engines, which she called 'flyology', predating the first design for an aerial steam carriage by several years. Aircraft are still a flawed technology compared to the anatomical perfection of birds, and jet engines damage the environment. We are a long way from silent flight or an engine which can overcome gravity without using fossil fuels.

p.52 In adult life, flight from her mother and her husband were never far from Ada's mind: her husband was at first the cock but later the crow.

p.56 'Woody Woodpecker' was one of my favourite cartoon characters – I loved his anarchic violent character, punching holes in man-made constructions. I only discovered recently that 'he' was voiced by a woman, who had to remain anonymous.

pp.57–60 M.C. Escher preferred the world of mathematics and science to the art world. In his woodcut 'Day and Night' white and black birds fly up from the flat polder land between two rivers. A landscape seen from a bird's eye view merges in the central part of the image with a changing tessellation, as the black birds evolve from the shadows of the white. Escher was fascinated by 'tessellations': repeated, interlocking forms like a jigsaw or Islamic tiles which metamorphose into each other. I became interested in 'tessellation' and how it might be applied to language.

The date of this picture, 1938, hints, in spite of Escher's inward emigration, at the imminent Nazi invasion – the V formation of geese in flight is the formation of military aircraft.

p.61 'Rudd- Duck' takes as its model the Byronic political epigram. It was written for a special issue of *Purge*, edited by Robert Hampson, in response to then Home Secretary Amber Rudd's attack on migrant workers.

p.62 'Written after walking…' is in an earlier Byronic mode, 'Written after swimming from Sestos to Abydos'. It celebrates, not heroic Greek swimmers, but those who risk their lives to fight airport expansion and climate change.

Unseen

If mathematics is the language of the unseen, this sequence explores various aspects of the 'unseen', which include computing, music, the imaginary, and the unseen matter of the universe. Equally important is human physiology, already evident in Ada's quest for a calculus of the nervous system with Andrew Crosse. Her own female body and illnesses were her 'experimental laboratory', and the medical profession's ignorance contributed to her early death.

pp.69–71 Epigram from Ada's letter to Babbage. He was irritated by her identification with fairies, but she persisted: 'It must be a very pleasant sort of thing to have a Fairy in one's service, mind & limbs! – I envy you! – I, poor little Fairy, can only get dull heavy mortals, to wait on me!' More seriously, she wrote of 'Fairyism' to Woronzow Greig her friend and confidant: 'she happens to have some of that very imagination which you would deny her to possess'. Fairies, like girls, would be diminished and sentimentalised in the 19th & 20th centuries – for example the *Flower Fairies* by Cecily Mary Barker. (See also *Troublesome things: a history of fairies and fairy stories*, Diane Purkiss, Allen Lane, 2000).

p.73 The lines on 'scena singing' are from Ada's letters about her singing lessons in London, which she tried to justify to her dismayed mother and husband. 'Seven Sisters Exit' was written for Rob Sheppard and a shared experience of London, the Underground, and pub music.

p.79 The 'hand of a housemaid' includes items in the Housemaid's Closet from the *Ashley Combe record book*, an inventory of every room in the house in the 1840s.

pp.80–81 'bubble vision' charts my experience of retinal deterioration and sight loss after eye surgery at Moorfields Hospital.

p.85 *Colour and vision: through the eyes of nature*, Steve Parker, Natural History Museum, 2016; Fay Bound Alberti, *This Mortal Coil*, OUP, 2016.

p.88 *An introduction to the history of psychology*, B. R. Hergenhahn, Wadsworth, 2008; 'Perception as an inference problem' Bruno A Olshausen in *The Cognitive Neurosciences*, MIT, 2013.

p.89 After reading *Neither the One nor the Other* with elizabeth james at the launch of *Out of Everywhere2*, edited by Emily Critchley, at XTL in August 2016.

p.91 Vera Rubin established that stars in the outer regions of galaxies move at similar speeds to those in the middle. Vast volumes of unseen matter, known as dark matter, provide additional gravitational grip on the stars.

pp.93–94 Will o' the Wisp, or *ignis fatuus*, was a common sight before the draining of the fens and marshes. By the time Ada used it to describe her difficulties with functional equations they were much rarer. JK is Dr James Kay, who wrote flirtatious letters to Ada, then hastily got married; JM is John Milton's *Paradise Lost*; ED – a reworking of Emily Dickinson's 'Those – dying then'. Mrs Lubbock was remembering incidents from before 1810 (*Norfolk: a ghost hunter's guide*, by Neil Storey). 'Joan the Wad' is a Somerset name for Will o' the Wisp. Scientists have attempted to recreate the right conditions for the spontaneous ignition of marsh gas.

p.95 Anthony Mellors introduced me to 'Irrlicht', from Schubert's *Winterreise,* and to Dersingham Bog. He uses Will o' the Wisp, with their 'strange light rising', in his *Gordon Brown Sonnets*, XXIV.

Search Ada

A search of 'Ada' from the first 20 pages of Google, in the order, though not strictly in the form, they occur: Wikipedia; ohbabynames.com; adainitiative.org; ada-books.com; ada.org.uk; computerhistory.org; tnmoc.org; adaslist.co; groups.engin.umd. umich.edu/CIS/course.des/cis400/ada/ada.html newyorker.com/tech/elements/ada-lovelace-the-first-tech-visionary wunderground.com/personal.../dashboard?ID=KOH**ADA**2 gnu.org/software/emacs/manual/ada-mode.html ferrovial.com/en/press-room/news/tunnel-boring-machine-ada-crossrail/ nytimes.com/books/97/03/02/lifetimes/nab-r-ada-appel. html/nickelinthemachine.com

'Ada is the most commonly used language for the mission-critical defense software, which includes weapons systems and performance-critical command, control, communications, and intelligence (C3I) systems... Hopes for broad commercial adoption of Ada have not been realized'. *Ada and Beyond: Software policies for the Department of Defense*, 1997 www.nap.edu/read/5463 (sent by A.R.)

Ada by Gertrude Stein, artwork by Atak, 2010. Design and typography by Melanie Gueret. Published by Nobrow Ltd, 62 Great Eastern Street, London EC2A 3QR (sent in the post by e.j.)

> Some one who was living
> was almost always listening
> Some one who was loving
> was almost always listening
> That one who was loving
> was almost always listening

Select bibliography & resources

Ada, the Enchantress of Numbers: a selection of letters of Lord Byron's daughter and her description of the first computer, edited by Betty Toole Strawberry, 1992

ADADA:landescape, by Tilla Brading & Frances Presley, Contraband, forthcoming

The Amazing World of M. C. Escher, National Galleries of Scotland, 2015

Ashley Combe and Culbone woods: a scoping report on the landscape, Debois Landscape Survey Group for Exmoor National Park 2015

Ashley Combe, Bratton Court & Sparkhayes record book, Lovelace Estate 1840s at Taunton Record Office

Base to Carry, by elizabeth james, barque, 2004

The Bride of Science: romance, reason and Byron's daughter, Benjamin Woolley, Macmillan, 1999

Byron Lovelace papers: at the Bodleian library, Oxford. Copyright Lord Lytton and Pollinger.

The Difference Engine: Charles Babbage and the quest to build the first computer, by Doron Swade, Viking 2000

The Emperor's New Mind: concerning computers, minds and the laws of physics, by Roger Penrose, OUP 1989

The Exmoor Society archive, library and resource centre
www.exmoorsociety.com

The House at Ashley Combe, by Barbara Milne n. p. 1985?

A preliminary survey of the former parish of Culbone, West Somerset by John Gamlin in Porlock library n.p. 1996?

Study of landslipped coastal slopes and moorland: Culbone woods Exmoor National Park 1991

The Thrilling Adventures of Lovelace and Babbage, by Sydney Padua, Penguin 2015

Acknowledgements

Poems have appeared in the following journals and anthologies and my thanks to all the editors concerned: *Shearsman,* Tony Frazer; *electric wood spectra*, Linda Kemp, Dan Eltringham & Leire Barrera-Medrano; *Plumwood Mountain*, Harriet Tarlo & Anne Elvey; *Molly Bloom,* Aiden Semmens; *Osiris*, Andrea Moorhead; *Purge*, Robert Hampson; *The World Speaking back... To Denise Riley*, Agnes Lehóczky & Zoë Skoulding; *Litmus*, Dorothy Lehane; *An Educated Desire: for Robert Sheppard at Sixty*, Scott Thurston; *Chicago Review*, Emily Critchley, Elizabeth Jane Burnett & Eric Powell.

Thanks to Lord Lytton and Pollinger Limited for permission to access the Lovelace Byron papers at the Bodleian Library, as well as Colin Harris and the Bodleian staff. For *ADADA: landescape* Tilla Brading and I visited Dr Helen Blackman at the Exmoor Society Archive in Dulverton; used local history sources and conducted interviews in Porlock; and were also assisted by Taunton Record Office.

My brother Derek, who contributed to the Ashley Combe project, died in 2015. Years ago, we were walking on Exmoor and he was talking endlessly about mathematical puzzles and the mysterious properties of numbers. 'It's crazy. We know what numbers are, we invented them, they're out there and yet we're discovering new things about them'. 'As if they have a life of their own'. 'Exactly'.

Also in memory of Derrick Woolf – architect, Coleridgean and poetry publisher.

I would like to thank everyone who helped with research and advice, especially my niece Nikki and her son Hal, Clive Bush, Moira Cassidy, Barbara and Tom Hall, Irma Irsara and John O'Leary, elizabeth james, George MacLennan, Anthony Mellors, Anna Reckin, Hazel Smith and my partner Gavin Selerie, who saw me through the unseen.